Finding Myself: A Psychological Expedition

Christopher Patterson

BookLeaf Publishing

India | USA | UK

Finding Myself: A Psychological Expedition
© 2022

Christopher Patterson

All rights reserved.

Presentation by *BookLeaf Publishing*

Web: www.bookleafpub.com

E-mail: info@bookleafpub.com

ISBN: 9789357444507

First edition 2022

A Glimpse of the Beyond

Beep
Beep
Beep
The heart monitor is counting down
Each beep is a day lost
Watching the internal clock's eternal tics and tocs
The cardiac television is constant, yet erratic
But it's time to change the channel
The beep crawls to a slow until all I can hear is static
Silence...
Patience...
The abundance of absence…
My senses must have taken a hiatus
Sensation is ripped from my lifeless hands
I remember everything, but nothing
I was born, yet I never existed
I am who I am, but who am I?
The never ending feelings of neutrality and nothingness consume me
Wait...what is that I see?

Is that a light?
My God, it's extraordinarily bright
Is it here to rescue me from this plight?
Its warmth envelops me
Hugging me like a long lost twin
The light begins to dim and I can finally see
Everso slightly, I gain clarity and I can identify
my savior
And it's...me
I am confused, yet intrigued
Mesmerized by the mystique of myself
I think it's trying to say something
Its mouth fixes itself in preparation for a
declaration
I am lost in awe and admiration, as if it
commands my observation
It opens its mouth so a pocket of air can escape
A necessary exhalation for an upcoming
statement
I'm growing impatient!
"Wa-"
Beep
Beep
Beep
My alarm clock goes off
I awaken and look over at my mirror
Everything is the same, but I'm a little off
My soul has been altered
Tampered with

My very being seems like a mystery
Certainty has been replaced with unfamiliarity
A spiritual coup
I look at my reflection and ask "Who are you?"

Unfulfilled Promises

"I promise to do better"
"I promise I'll never do that again"
"I promise that everything will be okay"
"I promise you will never feel this way again"

That insufferable phrase has been transformed
From a declaration to a cliche
A statement of change
Turned into a sign of complacency
And it will never be okay

Trust replaced with tiredness
Honesty replaced with deceit
Do you see a pattern here?
Nothing you say is concrete

Promises without action is manipulation
Clinging onto the hope that a promise will be
kept
That you'll stay true to your word
Waiting on a day that will never come

Break that unrelenting cycle and fly as free as a
bird

Don't promise me anything anymore
I all ever wanted was for you to be more
You swore and swore and swore and swore
But in the end, I realized I was being held
hostage
And I have to escape from this bondage no
matter what the cost is

It's Nice to Hear From You Again

It's been a while since we've last talked
How have you been?
I hope all is well
I've been waiting to hear from you again

Your voice is like music
Gliding over piano-like notes
The beauty in your glissando
The emotions your voice provokes
An elegance in your inflections
A culmination of vocal perfection

Your absence was noticed, my ears felt
neglected
My heart unfulfilled
My mind unstimulated
And my soul unsatisfied
But that healing agent you call your voice has
come to the rescue
Your signature sound discharges me from this
institution
Giving me the warmth I want

And the serenity I need

To others, your voice may not be special
But to me, it's all I could ask for
Talk to you soon
I can't wait to talk to you more

Sometimes

This imperfect flux of emotions rush into my
mind
Inconsistency is entombing me
Thinking of the haves and have-nots
Drowning in a sea of sorrow
Concerned about what I may think tomorrow

Imagining a world where sometimes, you care
Missing someone that doesn't miss you is a
different kind of prison
Trapped in a cell where walls are made of pieces
of myself
Is breaking out really what I want to do?

I want to let go, but what does it cost?
I want to stay, but what does it cost?
I can't decide
Sometimes, it's easier to ignore it than to face it
But when I put a face to my feelings
I am met with looks of discontent, but words of
praise

I'm perplexed
But I'd rather stay in this fantasy where
everything is okay

I'm not ready for reality
Not ready to confront my mania

Sometimes, my mind is my worst enemy
Sometimes, you are

Letting Go

I'll never get used to you not being here
I'll never get used to not being able to talk to you
Your mouth has been sewed shut, a mortician's
final blow
Locking your words inside of you

Death's guarantee is what makes it so petrifying
Its suddenness ripping you from me
Your heat and energy became cold
You're here
But you're not here

I used to think that we'd be together forever
Is my love powerful enough to wake you from
this eternal nap?
Can my passion make you hug me one last time?
Can my dedication give you enough strength for
a final kiss?
I can't let go of this

It doesn't get easier
And although I may seem stronger,
I am anything but
I wish God could give this one back

Eventually, we'll be back in touch
Until then, think about me and I'll think about
you
You'll love me and I'll love you, too
This isn't a "goodbye"
It's a "see you later"

Black Sheep

Conformity is the enemy of creativity
The threat on individuality is a threat on
diversity
On the road to establishing my own identity,
I am met with hostility

In an attempt to be different,
I become subject to abhorrence
Judgmental looks and comments become the
norm
The loss of camaraderie becomes acceptable
A declination of respect prompted by the
inclination of awareness

I am seen as less than human
As if I haven't been reminded of that for the last
400 years
We talk and scream, but to what avail?
A conversation can only be had if the other party
listens
These are the same principles in which we
fought for abolition

All we want are Three E's:
Equality

Equity
Emancipation
Without them, there is no "Us"
Only you and I
And there is too much at stake for a divide
We need a people
Not signs telling us that our lives don't matter

No more enmity
No more antipathy
After all, if there's no justice
There's no peace

Is It All An Illusion?

I look up in curiosity and acclaim
Attentive and intrigued
Calling out to Him in times of need
Often to the point of fatigue
But the phone is never answered
I'm forever leaving messages after the tone
Am I alone?

My faith is strong, but how far does blind faith
go?
Talking to something that won't talk back
Is there something wrong with me?
Can I take my prayers back?

I know that He works in mysterious ways
But has being blunt been rendered obsolete?
Decoding messages like a translator
Not noticing that they are incomplete

I have questions
Questions that I've never thought to ask before
Doubt cowers over me

Infecting my mind like it's pollution
And it makes me wonder
Is it all an illusion?

The Land of the Lost

Lost in this land of infatuation
Trying to discover myself in you
To the point where I can no longer distinguish
between us two
You guide and I comply
Like we're playing "Follow the Leader" with our
hearts

But you always take me to the same spot
I now know where to go
I follow the beacon to understanding
Cross the bridge of patience
Climb the mountain of trust
Swim the banks of honesty
I can hear your voice repeat these instructions
like a broken record
An unrelenting score of commands

But it's becoming harder to make amends when I
realize I forgot a step
I lost my footing and wandered, helpless

No sense of direction
Clinging onto any remaining familiarity like a
baby bird to its mother
The scarcity of hope is dehydrating and darkens
everything around me
A thirst only quenchable by thee
Your eyes give me the light so I can finally see

The path is clear again
It's not a mirage
This time, it's genuine
I've found my way back, and out of the blue, I
hear you say something new
"It's always been you"

Is It Over Yet?

The smell of hot dogs float into my nostrils
The sound of cars honking jolt me upright
The sight of infinitely tall skyscrapers that
extend past the clouds
The touch of the cold car door handle on a
winter day
The taste of hot chocolate as it singes the roof of
my mouth
This is my home

The smell of gunpowder invades my nose
The sound of loud bangs terrify and shake me
The sight of flashes in the distance warn me to
stay away from the windows
The touch of the hands of my loved ones as we
pray together for safety
The taste of my own blood as I bite my tongue
in angst
This is my home

Eyes on the Road

Rule One: Talk and act politely. Hostility could
cost you your life.
Rule Two: Keep your hands on the wheel unless
instructed to remove them.
Rule Three: Move slowly. I repeat, MOVE
SLOWLY!
Rule Four: Have all of your information ready to
present when requested.
Rule Five: Avoid eye contact.

Simple, right?
Oops, I almost forgot one.

Rule Six: Don't look intimidating.

The blacker the berry, the sweeter the juice
From where I'm from, I'd rather keep my juice
inside of my body
It's hard to see a target when it's on your back
So don't ever commit the heinous crime of
Driving while black

Navigating Happiness

Being happy is a mindset, not a state of being
One cannot simply be born with happiness, they
develop it
But don't give up too soon, you're right upon on
the precipice
You can choose to be happy
But don't expect for it to be snappy

Like art, being happy can't be rushed
Draw your own destiny with your own brush
There are no guidelines
No handbook, no how-to, no tutorial
No article to read, nor any editorial

We all go through a journey
But the one secret to being happy is focusing on
our own
Don't be so consumed by other paths that you
don't see the obstacles in yours
Never has a road been designed for you to take
detours

One small piece of advice:
Do not mistake being happy with being content
Settling doesn't lead to joy, it leads to toleration
Toleration leads to despair
Don't be afraid to clear your roadblocks
If others don't, you should care

Happiness is a priority
Never an option
And if you aren't happy
Proceed with caution

Why Do Good Things Happen to Good People?

Good vs. Bad
Right vs. Wrong
Topics so polar, they almost always appear
opposite one another
I propose, an idea, though
What if these qualities weren't on opposite sides,
but on a spectrum?
Now I know that's a popular idea to disconnect
from,
But for the sake of argument, humor me

Flip a coin
One side is heads, the others is tails
Some would say they are each others antitheses
But it's still the same coin, you see

I don't think you understand, yet.
It'll make sense soon, don't fret.

Happiness isn't really the opposite of sadness

The phrase goes "Ups AND downs", not "Ups
OR downs"
An upside down smile isn't a frown
Much like the opposite of a businessman isn't a
clown

Emotions don't come in absolute forms
That's why we scale things out of ten
One and ten being extremes, yet not
contradictory
Like how we think the future rivals history

Life can't be described in a single word
Life is a range of constantly changing emotions
So let's stop with the good vs. bad
We're all going through the motions

Existence revolves around the basis of
subjectivity
Objectivity is nonsensical
So let's stop with dichotomies
And get off of our pedestals

Sirens

Blaring, deafening
Unapologetically loud
Scolding me with its volume
Roaring like thunder from a storm cloud

It's crescendo can be heard from miles away
Gaining traction and octaves along the way
It's either a police car, ambulance, or the end of
days
I don't know if I should hide, help, or start to
pray

I can barely hear the sound of my own thoughts
And then suddenly
It stops

I look outside and, to no one's surprise, it's an
ambulance
Outside of the neighbor's house
But...the siren has been replaced with another
sound
Screaming
I see running
I can feel the panic in the air
So afraid, yet all I can do is stare

I can't help but think "What is going on over
there?"

The screaming continues
Each more blood-curdling than the last
I can't take this anymore
I get up, run outside, and ask
"What happened?"

I am met with silence
Moments after, there a gurney is rolled out of the
house
Atop it, a cold, pale figure lies motionless
The seemingly looping screams are persistent
I run back home, shellshocked
I hear that siren again
And instead of annoyance, it's trepidation
Fear of another fatal occasion

Utopia

I wish I lived in a world with no conflicts
No war, famine, disease, pollution, poverty
Wouldn't that be perfect?
Oh, how much fun that would be?
A world where happiness is always a guarantee!
Sounds like that's a world designed for me

This idea, though, is grounded in the realm of
science fiction
"Never will the real world fit such a description"
How are we so critical of an ideal?
Or is our faith in the human race as low as our
heel?

In either case, this idea isn't and can never be an
expectation
We must separate being idealistic with realistic
Fixing the world itself isn't the issue
We'd have to fix the species that inhabit it, too

We are imperfect creatures
We can be judgmental, angry, vengeful, hateful
I don't recall there ever being a war fought that
didn't involve us

So before we can tackle perfection, we must first discuss
Middle ground

The first step to solving a problem
Is admitting that there is one
Once we recognize that we're stunting our own growth,
Maybe we can move this topic to the non-fiction section of the library
Until then, we're not ready
I'll stick my imagination and wishes
We have highways, but unfortunately, we have forgotten how to build bridges

Time Is Of The Essence

I used to think that getting older was a curse
Punishment for trying to race time itself
But it's a blessing
Every wrinkle is a different story
Every ache is an old day of glory
A human time machine
Stocked to the brim with inventory

What I thought was dread became envy
Jealousy, stemming from the desire to be wise
I want experience, a lived life, a worry-free
lifestyle
And of course, social security
The elderly are the pinnacle of maturity

An endless supply of lessons
Banks of crystallized knowledge
So if you ever encounter those that have
obtained seniority
It never hurts to pay homage
To those responsible for the things you have
today

Giving You Your Space

I'm sorry if I overstepped a boundary
Why won't you talk to me?
Come on, I didn't mean it like that
I just want to chat

I've apologized already
What more do you want from me?
It was a mistake
What do you mean you want a break?

I get that you're upset, but is that what you really
want?
You want me to leave, but I won't
I won't leave you alone
I don't want to be on my own

Hello?
Fine, I'll go
I didn't mean to be that petty
Just let me know when you're ready

A Drive In The Car

It's raining
My head is leaning on the rear window
I look out of it, entranced in thought
Listening to Houston, Carey, and Dion
Water droplets hit the glass
Condensation builds up, creating a layer of fog
And now, I can barely see through the smog

I slide my hand across its cold surface to clear
the view
Using the glass as a canvas for my artistic
expression
I'm finding solace in this, otherwise gloomy, day
And all it took was taking the sunshine away
Now, everything feel like it's going to be okay

Death's Grasp

The end of this journey is upon me
I can feel his presence in the room
As if a shadow was without the figure projecting
it
It appears that darkness is imminent

The end of the beginning
The beginning of the end
He holds a scythe of death
A slice of life
I'm afraid of what the other side feels like.

I shake and shiver
Objecting to this transition
I don't want to lose this Earthly glow
But he has a firm grasp and won't let go
I beg and plead, but all I hear him say is
"No"

His emotionless voice and stone cold delivery
Resonate with me
It's my time to go
Will it hurt?
Where am I going?
I'm not ready

But I don't have a choice
I just hope I've left behind a legacy